#IndustryFamous

A WORLD-CHANGER'S GUIDE TO BECOMING
THE GO-TO PERSON IN THEIR INDUSTRY
BY LEVERAGING THE INTERNET

SHANEIL STEWART

#IndustryFamous

A world-changer's guide to becoming the

go-to person in their industry by leveraging

the internet.

By Shaneil Stewart

Copyright

CATALYST MEDIA HQ
FOR THE SMALL BUSINESS WITH A BIG HEART

Table of Contents

Preface

It was July 2014, and I was living what most people would assume was "the ultimate dream".

I was living in Paris.

Yes, the beautiful city of lights, the glitz and the glam... but something was terribly wrong.

I lived in Paris but I absolutely hated Paris.

I didn't hate Paris because Paris wasn't great, I hated it because it made it all too evident that I was nowhere near living the epic life I was meant for. I wanted more.

There I was studying for my Masters, working in social work, changing people's lives - by this point I had worked with over 600 clients helping them to transform their lives, find jobs, start business and even get ambassadorships. Yet, there I was stuck, unfulfilled, unhappy going through an identity crisis. Worse, I was broke.

I was barely scraping by and I was livid. It hurt having to know that deep inside I was called for greatness and all while feeling lost in the middle of the Atlantic in the peak of winter – frozen and stuck.

Being in that position, sadly, even made me begin to resent the powerful work I was doing. I remember thinking "How can I possibly help these people when I can barely even help myself". It's like I was gasping for air.

It's a painful thing when you want to change the world and help people but you can barely scrape by and help yourself.

As the summer semester was coming to a close, I knew I had to pack my stuff up and move on. I had $0 in my bank account and all I had was a train ticket to Italy to stay with my partner's family.

It was one of those train tickets where you get it on special and if you miss that specific train at that specific time you are doomed. Worse I still didn't even speak French and so there was no way I could even negotiate. I had to catch that train. I had no other choice.

And there I was rushing through the Nanterre University campus with my entire life packed into two 50 lb bags.

I remember rushing to catch my train and lugging these two 50lb bags with me, both bags bursting literally at the seams.

By this time, I had shaved my head off and died it platinum blonde in solidarity with my identity crisis. I was about to miss my train and it was at that moment that I cracked.

I stopped dead in my tracks. I threw everything on the ground with the force of giants. I looked up to the sky and started screaming at God.

I shouted, "I am meant for more than this! You called me to be great, you called me to touch lives and here I am can't even find 10 euros to grab a taxi" as tears filled my eyes. I honestly didn't even care about all the people at the basketball court steering at me. I squealed " I am about to miss my train and worse if I miss this train I am homeless!"

I continued barely articulating my words, "I want to change the world so bad and I deserve to be compensated well for it".

It was as if the entire earth stood still as I pointed to the sky beyond the tree in front of me "you fix this and you fix this NOW!" I demanded angrily at God.

But you know as they say ask and it shall be given. I continued to scurry along to the train station and thankfully in nick of time as I swung my bags into the train, *ding* the doors closed.

I sat on the train with a determination I had never experienced before, I was going to fix my life. I was going to change the world AND make money too.

Within 2 days I discovered online coaching. It was the perfect way for me to change lives and help people and continue the transformative work I was doing as social worker, but this time I could REALLY be compensated for it. I could change lives and not be broke all at the same time.

The internet was my answer!

Well in all honesty, I would love to say I rode off into the sunset and became a millionaire in 5 minutes. But unfortunately, it doesn't work like that. Well at least for me it didn't.

The online coaching world was a whole other ball game and I was about to learn just how much sweat and tears it would take to put that concept of being successful online into a reality and just how challenging "changing the world and being compensated" was going to be.

You see the coaching industry was reported in 2016 to be the second largest growing industry in the US, second to technology therefore you can only imagine the high level of competition there was (seemingly).

How on earth could I stand out? How could I position myself as the expert? Why should someone work with me? And why on earth should they pay me thousands of dollars? Worse I had no idea where to even start.

I could tell from the get go...

This... was going to be tough!

You see to change the world and be paid by using the internet, you need a formula. And for those out there who are from the entrepreneurial spirit, it can be quite easy sometimes.

But for others of us, especially those of us from the school of "helping people should be free", it is a journey... or even more like a roller coaster ride

There are certain steps, and processes you must go through in order to guarantee your success.

And that's exactly why I am writing this book because the truth is dear world-changer, you can stand out, you can be the go-to person in your industry and you most certainly can become wildly profitable doing it too!

You simply need a formula.

It took me 2 years of trial and error and failing and falling to get from 1 client a year and having only family and friends like my stuff to now:

- Having a tribe of well over 11,324 people and growing from 27 countries.
- Building a brand and business that people can rely on.
- Having raving fans who tell their friends about my work and have my programs spread like wild fire.
- Creating consistent income and knowing I will never have to work for someone else ever again unless I want to.
- Having clients travel from LA all the way to London to come to my live events.
- Being able to have a book like this in a YOUR hand wherever you are in the world.

And that is what this book is about. If I can do it, a female millennial from the tiny island of Jamaica with an accent, who lost her mom at 15, and who slept in lockers in train stations, then so can you!

If you want to change the world, now is your time.

If you want to create consistent income without ever having to work for someone else again, now is your time.

If you are ready to stand out and become the go-to expert in your industry and have a tribe of raving fans who believe in what you do, cheer you on and yes even invest in your work- now, my friend is the time. And that to me my love is what it means to be truly #IndustryFamous™.

Acknowledgements & Dedications

This book is dedicated to my sister Tamoy, you are truly the inspiration behind why I do what I do and I am so grateful to have your love and encouragement every step of the way. Continue being the light you are.

I want to also thank the love of my life, Carlo for putting up with my moodiness and being there to encourage me as I wrote this book and as I spent years in self-discovery and learning. I have change probably 50 times since you met me and yet you have shown me what unconditional love truly means. Thank you.

To my father, Neil, thank you for being my biggest supporter. Thank you for being there and thank you for always praying for me and encouraging me and for being the greatest example of a world-changer to me. Your love and guidance has changed my life and for that I am forever grateful.

I would like to thank all my family members and friends, for believing in me and for expecting nothing less than the best. Your faith in me has pushed me to experience what my "best self" is.

To my clients and past clients, thank you for allowing me to be a part of your life and for allowing me to help you step even more into the best version of you – the Rock Star you!

And most importantly, I want to thank God for granting me the courage to write this book and calling it #IndustryFamous™ even when it felt it was the hardest and scariest thing I have ever done.

Introduction - The Industry Fame Formula ™

I don't think as a society we've ever been more blessed and privileged than today. I know it's easy to get bombarded by the negativity across the world but do you realize that you can stay RIGHT where you are, right now, in the comfort of your bedroom, wearing PJs and reach millions of people from across the globe in an instant.

It's more than possible with things like social media, email marketing and live streaming!

Nowadays, you don't have to wait for Oprah to call for you to become the go-to expert and finally have credibility in your industry (even though of course Oprah calling certainly won't hurt... which by the way

Oprah, if you are reading this hit me up *winks*).

The fact is with technology today, you can literally create a brand and a movement by leveraging the internet that could potentially make YOU the next Oprah or whatever your industry's version of that is.

Today, world-changers and people with massive missions don't need BBC or NBC to call us to give us the chance to have our own television shows with millions of viewers anymore – we can start our own.

The same goes for radio – we can start podcasts or online radio shows and stream to listeners in every nook and cranny.

World-changers like us no longer need to rent out arenas to host live events because now with two clicks of a button, we can host our own webinar online with thousands of people from every corner of the globe, as long as they have an internet connection.

This IS the time of the catalysts, the world-changers, the rule breakers and the people with a message who are ready to let their voices roar. This is your time to be the go-to expert in your industry by leveraging the internet. This is your time to become #IndustryFamous™.

You see, I don't believe in coincidences and you most certainly aren't reading this book by mistake. I believe your soul has called out for more. You've been looking for a way to become epic, to be the legend and icon that you know you were born to be and let's face it, this is your chance.

You don't have to settle for being the best on your street anymore (unless that's what you want). You have before you the opportunity to literally become the best in the world! Hands down.

Don't believe me? Well take it from all the 15-year-old cover artists on YouTube who have since scored major recording deals and TV show appearances.

Or the vine celebrities who now have world tour comedy shows.

If they can become superstars who are totally rocking it out on social media and spreading their message - Why not you?!

Even though this hope of rising to the top sounds all glamourous, I must admit there is a reason most people never become successful.

There is a reason why so many fail and face what I like to call the 1 hit wonder syndrome.

Some people never get the glory, and worse some who do, they never maintain it. They strike gold and then they run out.

They are back to the shell of what their lives used to be, having the taste of victory be overshadowed by the memories of could haves, should haves and would haves.

They lacked 1 thing.

A formula.

You see the people who you see being successful online and staying successful, they follow a formula. Whether knowingly or unknowingly they follow a step by step process for lasting success. I call it:

The Industry Fame Formula ™

The industry fame formula is what allows rock stars on the rise, world changers and catalysts, and legends in the making to not just achieve the success they crave, but to maintain it by having their names printed in the history books.

It's the process wherein your name becomes written on the sands of time.

This formula has 5 pillars but at the simplest level has two basic steps. It's Marketing + Mindset (both of which are covered in the subsequent chapters of this book).

I know, it's a simple formula but before you go closing the book, let me say this isn't the kind of marketing they teach in university.

You see this is a WHOLE other ball game and while some of the core principles may be the same, the execution certainly is not.

Failure to execute correctly can result in you getting blocked, banned, reported and even marked as spam. You know we all have that one friend who messages us on Facebook and asks us to join their team or their downline and we both know once they do that we never look at them the same again.

Or who knows, maybe you are that friend and let me just say your friends are secretly giving you the side eye. Now I am not bashing network marketing, the model certainly has it's benefits, in fact I have clients and friends who do it, however, if you are that spammy friend everyone avoids like the plague, then you've got to keep reading because when you're marketing online, the game completely changes – you need a formula.

In Part 1 of this book when we talk about marketing online and becoming the go to person in your industry, we'll talk about:

1. Building a massive reach of ideal clients and customers, a tribe of raving fans who want what you are offering

2. Building up your credibility (I share 5 steps in that chapter of how to rev up your credibility TODAY!). If you want to be the "Go-To" expert you've got to have credibility.

3. Connecting and engaging and having people connect and engage with you - I share with you several tips to do this too, along with 1 thing that I think is the most important that many of us forget to add into our efforts online.

4. After you've gained all this credibility and gotten all these people to know you, I would highly recommend you monetize.

    This is of course optional, but I recommend it because if you can do work you love and never worry about the bills – why not!?

    You get to wake up every day, change people's lives AND be compensated too and in this book as a part of the Industry Fame Formula™ I'll take you through the marketing steps when it comes to monetizing your mission and your message online as a world-changer because I personally don't believe any world-changer should have to face the "Starving Artiste Syndrome".

5. And lastly in the part of this book about Marketing, we talk about innovation and how to stay relevant in the ever changing and over-crowded online world.

In Part 2 of the book we talk about Mindset and I'll dive into the reason most people never get the success they dream of and why those who achieve it sometimes don't maintain it.

I don't want you to be a one-hit wonder and so in Part 2 of the book we talk about ways to prevent it by using mindset.

Dispelling the Controversy of Being Rich & Famous

Before I start dishing the goods and sharing with you the actual steps to becoming #IndustryFamous™, let's address the elephant in the room, let's dispel the controversy around the topic of being rich and famous.

"Fame" is a very controversial topic, just like the topic of being rich.

People get very triggered when they hear about it. However, there is a lot of forward movement when it comes to entrepreneurs looking at money in a positive light. Especially here in the online entrepreneurial world where there is a lot of talk about the money story, law of attraction, abundance and manifesting.

Obviously because if someone is in business they would generally like to make some money, if not they would probably just go and work for somebody else. Most entrepreneurs want to make money and they want to make it in their own way and on their own terms.

And just as in many circles, we hear people say negative things about rich people all the time. Rich people are mean, Rich people are wicked or rich people are evil.

We hear members of society share these kinds of views about wealthy people all the time and so when you come into the online entrepreneurial world and you are trying to make money you must think about wealth differently.

You must view money differently.

However, while the story of money is controversial, for entrepreneurs it's also a necessity and so for the sake of this book we will be talking about the other controversial topic that I believe all entrepreneurs (especially the ones with big missions to change the world) need to focus on too.

I'm talking about FAME.

Fame is another thing that society bashes. We often hear things like "famous people are snobbish" or maybe you've heard they are stuck up or they think they're better than people or they're not nice, they're mean. And sometimes we even hear that famous people end up unhappy and they even become addicts.

Thus, maybe you want to be visible, you have a message and a mission and you want to change the world. You want to stand out and become what I like to call Irresistible in Your Industry. You want to be the Crème de la Crème.

You have a message, you have a calling, you have something that the world needs to see, needs to feel, they need to experience it and unfortunately because people in society see fame as being bad, you have been playing small.

You've been hiding yourself, you've been hiding your desires, you've been hiding your dreams, and you've been trying not to take up too much space. You've been trying not to be too loud or too out there because you don't want people to think you think you're better than them.

You don't want to be judged, trolled, hated or criticized.

But let me tell you something, you becoming famous, is your number 1 responsibility if you are a catalyst, a world-changer and if you want to leave a legacy in this world. You also get to choose whatever degree of Fame lights you up (because there are different degrees of fame).

If you're not famous in your industry, if nobody knows you even exist, there's no way you can expect to get your message out there.

Let me ask you a question. Do you think Mother Teresa was famous? Yes, yes, she was.

What about Dr. Martin Luther King, do you think he was famous? Okay.

Nelson Mandela? Precisely.

Oprah? Yes.

So many incredible iconic people and if they did not have their fame they would not have the platform to create the change in the world that they did.

They would not be the catalysts that they were.

Let's consider Gandhi, Mohammed Ali and yes even the Dalai Lama.

Hold up… what about Jesus? He did say after all "Go Ye Therefore Into The World And Teach All Nations…" – Mathew 28:19.

So what are you waiting for?

If people don't know you how can you expect them to work with you and I'm talking specifically to the people who are trying to change the world with your services or your products and your programs. You're trying to do something big.

I am not talking about the people who want to chase fame to feel validated. That is not what this book is about.

I'm talking about people who want to stand out in their industry, they want to captivate, they want to be number one, they want to be the best thing since sliced bread in their field, because they know they can make a difference.

With that said, let me just say for every day that you are not famous, for every day that you make yourself small, for every day you hide your flame and squint yourself and try not to take up too much space, there are people out there who are suffering.

I know it's a hard pill to swallow, but sometimes we need a little tough love.

And I can say this now because I know where I am coming from, and I know that's where you may be right now.

You see, I remember back in 2014 it was December and I went to this conference with this high level multi 7 figure earner coach that I hired and there were 200 of us in the room.

I flew halfway across the world, I didn't even have the money, I had to put everything on a credit card but I had a dream and I knew I wanted more for my life and I was going to get myself in the room.

So, I flew halfway across the world to go to this conference to be in this community of high vibrational women... and do you know what I did the entire time?

Every time the coach would say go mingle and meet each other and network, I went and I hid in the bathroom.

I literally went and I HID in the bathroom.

I completely choked up. Instead of forming friendships, I would stay in the stall and wait until the crowd died down, listen for the final flush and then I would run back to my hotel room and hide some more until the next session started.

I played small, played safe. I didn't want to be too loud and I didn't want to be too out there. I didn't want to show up too much, I didn't want to shine too much.

I thought, what if I wasn't good enough? What if they don't like my accent? What if they thought I was too young or immature?

Do you know what happened?

I was completely overlooked.

Not by the people there but by my own self.

I was overlooked by my purpose. There were people who needed to meet Shaneil, for example you reading this book right now, who would have never met me had I stayed there, hiding and playing small.

However, the moment I decided to become visible. To stand out and to be #IndustryFamous™ and to be known and to be seen and to be heard, and to give myself permission to shine. I could finally change people's lives.

By deciding to shine, I could light the path for other world changers and help to change how they saw themselves since they were six years old, when they were bullied at school.

By allowing myself to take centre stage in my industry I could help people move from that place of fear and hiding to finally showing up in their life as the icons that they are meant to be.

The moment I stopped hiding and playing small, that's when I stepped into my purpose and realized that I'm here to help people with their mindset AND their marketing too, because yes, believe me Mother Teresa had a marketing strategy.

So, I'm taking a chance. I'm writing this book because I want to challenge how we, as a society, view fame.

Fame is the number one responsibility of any catalyst. Therefore, if you are here and you are reading this book and nobody knows about you and you have a message to share, now is the time for you to step up. Now is the time for you to step out and become #IndustryFamous™.

We are about to dive into this book where I share with you some steps to get you started and help you to claim your status as a total Industry Rock Star.

I want to invite you to ask yourself a couple of questions:

- What do you really want to be known for?
- What is that thing that you have on your heart since you were a kid?

I can imagine that all your life you knew you were called for something great, or maybe you just recently had a major epiphany, and maybe you don't know what that "something great" is, but you know in your heart that there is something there.

As we go through this book, I want you to really ask yourself what that is because just by you gaining awareness about what that is for you, you open yourself up taking another step and another step.

It's called momentum.

One step and another step and eventually you do get the chance to become that #IndustryFamous^{TM} person that you know you're meant to be.

I want you to see in this book that fame and being famous, being #IndustryFamous^{TM} is your number one responsibility.

The Industry Fame Formula ™

PART 1 – The Marketing

Fame in it's simplest definition means to be known by many people. Therefore, it's safe to say if this book is going to teach you how to become famous in your industry, I couldn't possibly leave out the part where you create a massive reach of raving fans who want what you are offering.

Please note: For this section I do have a bonus PDF worksheet that I made just for you to help walk you through some of what we will cover in this chapter. You can get your free PDF along with some other juicy bonuses at www.irresistibleinyourindustry.com/industryfamousbookbonus/

Let's dive in!

Step 1 – Pic 1 Thing You're Going to Be Famous For

Choose the 1 thing that you want to be known for.

Just think about what kind of doctor you would want operating on your brain. Do you want a General Practitioner who can diagnose everybody or do you want someone who specialises in brain work?

I am sure most if not all of us would choose the later.

Why? Because we see them as the expert and so by choosing 1 category or niche you begin to position yourself as an expert.

Let's look at a few of the world's most famous catalysts:

- Mother Teresa – Famed for Serving the Poor & Destitute
- Dr Martin Luther King – Famed for His Work in The Civil Rights Movement
- Bill Gates – Famed for His Work in Technology and Computers
- Nelson Mandela – Famed for His Fight Against Apartheid
- Albert Einstein – Famed for His Work in Physics

Now of course none of these living legends only did that one thing, I am sure they knew how to do tons of other things too.

For example, Dr King knew how to negotiate and was a great orator but it was his stance during the civil rights movement that catapulted him and allowed him to even have the platform for negotiations and world famous speeches.

Most legends became famous for ONE thing and remember success leaves clues so take this lesson from their work, there is no need for you to try to reinvent the wheel, so my task to you is to pick that 1 thing that you want to be known for.

Step 2- Pick 1 Person To Help (Your Audience)

Now that you've bit the bullet and picked that one thing you're going to be known for, your next step is to pick the audience. If you are going to build a tribe of raving fans and supporters, you must know who they are.

I know as world-changers and catalysts there are so many times we want to change the world and we think we should start there... "The World". We want to help any and everybody and we want to do any and everything.

However, if you pay very close attention to all the catalysts of old, and all the legendary and iconic world-changers of yester year, none of them changed the world by helping everybody or by doing everything.

They each had 1 area where they excelled, and that one area is what made them memorable. By them shining in 1 area and staying in their zone of genius, they ended up leaving an indelible mark on the entire world any way.

Therefore, even though this advice may feel counter intuitive to that big heart of yours, I want to encourage you to help ONE person, or at least one specific type of person or category of person.

Ask yourself the following:

- Who can you relate to?
- Who do you have an association or connection with and know how or where to find them?
- How are they similar to you?
- What traits do you have in common with them?
- What are their secret desires? Their dreams? Their goals?

That is your tribe! And again if you need more help to work through this remember to check out your book bonuses where I have a PDF worksheet that walks you through these questions. You can grab your bonuses by going here:

www.irresistibleinyourindustry.com/industryfamousbookbonus/

Now that you know what you do and who you serve, your next step is going to be building your credibility and actually mastering that area.

Before you go out there and totally rock it out and write your name in the sands of time as the best XYZ in your industry and potentially the world, you have got to be good at what you do or be willing to work at it.

That means you must build up your credibility and practice mastery.

Credibility

The internet is the one place where we can easily separate the sheep from the goats. If we are looking for a service or a solution and we find you, and you disappoint us, then we simply head on over to our trusted friend Google and find someone better.

The internet is not like small town living where even if that 1 doctor sucks you've got to use him any way because he's the only doctor in your area.

Not online.

Online people have choices and they are going to choose the service or product that resonates with them and that they can trust.

It is therefore your responsibility to position yourself in the consumers mind as that trust worthy source.

In fact, online with things like social proof, testimonials and reviews, sometimes people don't even get to give you a chance, much less a second chance, and so you've got to come good.

I remember sending out a survey to my clients once and asking them what they would want to see on my website to decide if I was the coach for them.

Of all the respondents, a resounding 70% of them said testimonials, or stories of other clients.

The other 30% said something along the lines of "can you really help me", which of course with testimonials and reviews you'll be able to show that with ease.

Even though testimonials are a great credibility booster, testimonials are just 1 form of credibility.

Others forms may be things like certifications and accolades, or even just feedback from your community, so things like comments and likes and other forms of engagement.

Even the use of referrals by influencers or other people they trust will go a long way in boosting your credibility.

Just think about the time you bought something because a friend bought it and they told you it was amazing, or the time your friend sent you that funny video or meme to watch.

In all honesty, sometimes, the thing disappoints in the end, sometimes the cat video just isn't that funny, but just because a friend recommended it you stick with it rather than trying to seek out something else.

Consumers like to be comfortable when making decisions and so the more ease you can provide in the process through being credible, the more successful it'll be in the end.

I must say though, while all these forms of credibility are good. **Nothing beats giving people an actual transformation.** Give them a result.

Giving them great value or a fabulous experience is the most effective form of credibility you could ever create.

Why?

Because at the end of the day, that person becomes their own testimonial. They experienced you and your brand and your message first hand, and those are the things that create evangelists for your brand.

I know it's common practice to think that we should just go into content over load and churn out 3 blog posts a day, 10 videos a week, and 500 pics a month for Instagram and so on.

However, the truth is, that's horrible advice – especially when the content is mediocre and subpar.

I hate reading these posts that talk about, how often you should post, because the fact is the online consumer can see through the fluff, they can feel how ingenuine it is. And while I believe you should post daily and stay in front of your audience, I would honestly prefer you give me 1-2 quality pieces of life changing content a week, rather than daily garbage.

It sounds tough but I know you can relate because it not only looks bad, but it ruins your credibility.

I am very passionate about this because I used to post daily garbage too.

#CONFESSION

I used to post just because I thought I had to. I was posting content that wasn't aligned. Things that didn't feel good to me but just going through the motions and checking off my to do list every day to say "yes I posted" or tweeted or whatever platform it was.

You know what it got me? No clients, a ruined reputation, my business started to feel like a chore and I had people unsubscribe from me (as if it wasn't hard enough getting people to sign up in the first place).

It also put me in a very dark place where I began to feel I wasn't "good enough" or that no one wanted what I was offering.

However, that wasn't true. People did want what I had offer, I was just going about it all wrong... I was going about it in a creepy stalker girl kind of way and so they created the online version of a restraining order against me.

Can somebody say #blockparty... ouch!

So, here's what you do instead:

1. Pick a day each week and call it your content creation day – Mine is on Tuesdays. And when I have big launches I do half days on Saturdays too. By picking a day you are making time to create good quality content without feeling overwhelmed by all the other responsibilities and tasks you have to do. It prevents you from creating rushed content that sucks.

2. Brainstorm content ideas that truly help people (not just random info they can source on google or Wikipedia, actually put some thought into it). Be inspired and let your creativity FLOW. I throw a 1 woman dance party and listen to my reggaetón party mix and it soups me up with ideas.

3. Add a little personality, in other words your personal story or an example or anecdote and yes maybe even a little humour or vulnerability too. Maybe even throw in some diagrams to illustrate. Just please for crying out loud, make it fun.

4. Have a set schedule when you share this juicy content and stick to it. With technology, you can even schedule

your posts out a month in advance. That way you can still post daily if you want but at least it's not dry lifeless content and at least you don't have to be perpetually glued to your computer screen. Plus, your credibility stays high, people rely on you for epic content and you also just managed your time really really well.

5. Have a call to action to engage people. Remember in the beginning of this chapter I shared that there's power in the community so when you get people to engage with you and your content and other community members, that totally revs us your credibility. So say things like, leave a comment, tag a friend,

share this, tell me what is your biggest takeaway etc..

Mastery

What do Olympic Gold Medallists, Dr Martin Luther King Jr, Kim Kardashian and Mother Theresa all have in common?

To put it plainly – work ethic, dedication and support.

They had a goal and they worked towards it day in day out. It became their obsession.

They knew they had a mission and they were determined to make it happen no matter what. They didn't let judgement and fear of what people think and fear of failure hold them back. They committed to MASTERY, and they surrounded themselves with people who understood and supported their mission.

In the 1st chapter of this book I spoke about the one hit wonders. The people who strike gold and then run out. The people who are gone with the wind and who have been blown away from our thoughts as the chaff blows in the wind.

They simply stopped pushing, they chose where they are versus to strive continuously towards the mark of a higher calling. And nothing is wrong with that but if you want to be at the top and stay, you will have to strive.

You have to want the new life more than the comfort of the old.

Of course, being an influencer and having legend like success I assume is stressful to an extent, but so is living less than your calling.

And I get it, not everyone is meant to be a legend, of course not. That's why some people get on the brink of success and cease to rise, however if you want to get the success and maintain it, if you want to be the Go-To person in your industry, you have to have a very strong work ethic.

It can't be that every notification on Facebook throws you into a 3 hour long spiral of distraction. Get a grip!

You may even have to be willing to sacrifice sleep sometimes, not every day but some days you honestly may, I am just being honest.

You may be required to say no to some things and delay gratification while others are off frolicking in the meadow and instead of joining in, you are working.

Yes, you have to have laser sharp focus on your goal and that may mean no distractions regardless of who the person is.

Yes, you even have to invest financially in the things that are going to get you to your goal, whether it be coaching or mentorship or even an up level in your technology.

Yes, you even have to be able to receive hate or criticism but keep moving regardless.

Yes, you have to know the competition is there without getting into comparison and without being side tracked from your mission because of watching others.

Yes, you have to choose to become a master.

Beyoncé as a child practiced running on a treadmill in heels, and if that isn't dedication I don't know what is.

I know it can sound daunting and it may sound like an uphill battle, doesn't it?

But it only has to be that way when you try to do it on your own. My advice to you is to make sure you have someone in your corner.

Every catalyst has a catalyst. Whether it's a coach or mentor or mastermind partner; after all Dolce had Gabbana, Beyoncé had Matthew Knowles and even Jesus had 12 disciples.

That support is something I make sure all my own clients have because rising to the top is easier when you have a community of rock stars by your side and a mentor who is there to encourage you when (not if, but when) the tough times come.

Now you've gained credibility and mastery, it's time to create lasting engagement with your tribe and truly build up that credibility by building up your community.

What if you had 10,000 subscribers but they were all unengaged?

Imagine posting to your 10,000 followers and having 1 or 2 people like your post and having only your biz bestie comment. Believe me it happens, and I see it all the time online.

cough it used to happen to me *cough*

Really though, there are times when I'll go onto a Facebook page of an entrepreneur with hundreds of thousands of followers and when I look at their posts, I see 2 likes!

It used to shock the beJesus out of me... until I realised why.

You see social media is a relationship.

And when you see it as a relationship this will happen way less.

We have to realise that followers are actual people. Actual human beings with lives, and feelings, and dreams, and aspirations and emotions.

And even though you can schedule out your social media posts a year in advance (and yes sometimes I schedule my posts too), however, if your posts are dry and unemotional or just basic and vague and valueless...

Why on earth would anyone want to engage with it?!

I would prefer to see you post once a day and post something of real value, something that connects me with you, rather than for you to just say "yahoo, I posted 3 times today" but all three posts are utter rubbish.

Do I have some rubbish posts?

Of course!

I'm human, but I would hope that not all my posts are rubbish. All posts, every single day... all the time.. consistent rubbish, just 100% rubbish??

One word....

Eew.

So for me here are my top rules for social media engagement:

1. Give a hoot.

You have to CARE about people and show that you care. Be inspiring and actually share messages that people want to hear. I'll give you an example from my own Instagram account. This one photo had over 1000 likes and 52 comments.

In this example, you can see that the post I wrote was thoughtful, and creative. I knew my ideal clients were struggling with wanting to bloom, and yet here was this flower showing me and them that we can give ourselves permission to shine, guilt free.

This picture was taken from the garden in the back yard. I didn't need a fancy photoshoot, or snazzy wording. It was just clear, and pure and from the heart.

It didn't even have a whole bunch of hashtags. Simple, and sweet and to the point.

When you CARE about your tribe, and when you put out content that speaks to their soul, they feel it and that is where engagement starts.

Think of a relationship, and when a couple gets engaged. This is the point in their relationship when they are saying I love you, I want to spend the rest of my life with you, and engagement online on one hand may not seem as deep, but on the other hand, it really of is.

Don't be afraid to express care for your audience. It will distinguish you from the others and help to position you as that go-to expert.

2. Be YOU. Be vulnerable.

If you are crazy, weird, moody – be that!

I was watching a video on YouTube the other day by a guy named PewDiePie who has over 50 million YouTube subscribers. Maybe you've heard of him.

In the video, he talks about all the false positivity online and how everything must seem honky dory all the time and how much it irritated him.

He even admitted that he was caught in that trap too, where he would come online and pretend to be all happy and then as soon as the recording stopped, he went right into a bad mood and hated how he felt.

Now when I say don't go to the next extreme where you are a Debby Downer, miss complainer and always in a bad mood, because nobody wants that either, people have their own problems and definitely don't need you to be all up in their grills with your pain.

Ain't nobody got time for that!

Nonetheless, when people see that you are a human, with real emotions, with insecurities and vulnerabilities, they trust you. They feel like they know you. And they even like you.

Why do you think the Kardashian-Jenner empire was such a massive success?

Because people got to see them behind all the glitz and glam and make up and gorgeousness.

They got to see the mess. The tears, the sadness, the confusion. Emotions that we can all relate to. The sibling rivalry, the heart breaks, the vulnerability.

Their fans got to see the behind the scenes and just how much they worked.

And you don't have to go to the extreme of videotaping your messy life, but you still SHARE your mess. Your message is in your mess. Be vulnerable and share your story.

Oprah shares openly her past with teenaged pregnancy. Tony Robbins shares openly having to go without food. We like them and they inspire us because we see where they are now and just how much they have grown. It's a message to us that we can rise too.

So, share your story. Share yourself with your audience and don't be afraid to be vulnerable.

I know some of us are afraid to share ourselves and our stories. I can totally relate. I used to say "can't I just give them the tips!!". But the truth is that made me un-relatable. **And even if I was the best in my industry, I became instead the best kept secret**. Because no one knew me. I was way too impersonal.

I remember sharing my story for the first time in early 2015. I opened up about my quarter life crisis, and how I had gained a lot of weight, and how I would curl up in my dark room for days and just stuff my face with Pringles and Frozen Pizza.

I shared my story of when my friends would call and I wouldn't answer, and when they rang the doorbell I pretended I wasn't home.

I shared that story in a video for the first time and someone saw it and reached out to work with me the same day. She wasn't even on my email list, she saw the video and in that moment, she herself was curled up in the dark of her room wondering what to do with her life.

Just by sharing my story I got my first ever paying client, I finally got to call myself a real coach and a real entrepreneur because I really had people I was helping and I was getting paid for it.

So share your story, and be yourself. You'll have people reaching out to you and commenting and liking and sharing.

3. Have 1 solid call to action

I remember hearing the quote "A confused mind always says no" and the truth is when you have a piece of content and you give someone 5000 things to do... they end up doing 1 thing – leaving.

Instead of saying like my page, comment, share, tag a friend, sign up for my webinar, follow me hear, subscribe to me there, watch my video and join my group all in 1 breath... your audience screams "ahhhhhh" and runs away.

Instead, have 1 solid call to action and you will drastically increase the chance of that person following your instructions.

So, your call to action could be "leave a comment below and share what questions you have". That allows them to respond, which builds engagement. When you reply it builds the engagement even more.

In those follow up conversations you help the person – give them a transformation or a result (remember the best credibility is when someone experiences you for themselves).

Maybe they had a question, you simply answer it and if you had a resource then in your response to them you could have another call to action for them to get the resource or whatever that other step is.

In this way, at each stage of the relationship they have 1 decision to make, because you made 1 call to action.

4. Don't be afraid to repel people

I'm truly tired of seeing powerful world-changers with big hearts and big dreams and big goals, stuck beneath co-dependency and people pleasing.

There is this phrase that says "If you stand for nothing you'll fall for anything" and so my best advice to you is not to fear rejection.

Don't be afraid to repel people. The fact remains that there are over 7 billion people on the planet and all of them are most not your tribe.

Go where you are wanted and be open to repelling the unideal people who don't get your message anyway.

Back when I was 18, I had a friend who would talk to me about manifesting. However, at that time I was thoroughly brainwashed to think that any that that used that kind of language was some sort of blasphemy.

As he would explain I would be very judgemental and closed off and would even go as far as saying things like, "I really hope you find God".

Looking back now, all I can say is... Wow!

Really looking back now I was really closed minded in that situation. However, at that time I could only understand what he was saying based on what I knew. I saw his words through my own tinted glasses.

It wasn't until years later when I realised that manifesting was not "evil", and that the bible was filled with miracles and manifestations. Even just by praying and receiving what you asked for, that is you manifesting.

Nonetheless, at age 18, living in the Caribbean and being deep in the Pentecostal church, I just couldn't fathom that thought.

And so it's the same with your message. Some people don't get it, and some people won't get it. That's not your business. They will get it in due time if they are meant to.

Your role is to make sure the message goes out and that the seeds are planted.

People have free will and they won't all want what you are offering. I know it hurts because you really want to help, but deal with it, it's the burden of the blessed.

Jesus was ostracised for his beliefs, and so too were the Wright brothers when they said we could fly..

And so too Benjamin Franklin when he discovered electricity.

And in all honesty the list could truly go on.

Anybody who is anybody was misunderstood at some point in their life and so don't let that stop you.

Don't be afraid to speak your truth.

As Clarissa Estes says in the book Women Who Run with The Wolves "You have to howl so your pack with hear you". Speak your truth my love, and speak it loud, strong and proud and know that the people who are meant to hear it, will come running!

Those are the people you want to engage with your material anyway.

And worse case you get some trolls? That's what the block button was made for.

Don't you just love technology?!

Let's face it, trends change, social media evolves, platforms rise and most certainly fall and so to be consistently visible, you have to think like a chameleon.

You must always be on the ball, always have your ears to the ground and stay on top of what's happening in the world regarding technology.

Here's exhibit A – Myspace.

Here's exhibit B – Hi5

Both platforms at some time in the past where the TOP social networking platforms. You'd add your friends, share photos and keep up to date with all the latest news and happenings.

But now? Who cares... not to be mean but when I say the word "MySpace" to teenagers I know, they look at me as if I'm from another planet, and when I talk to friends about MySpace, they get this reminiscent look on their face because they didn't even remember such a platform existed.

It doesn't mean Myspace wasn't effective, in fact, a lot of creatives and entrepreneurs built massive influence using MySpace.

However, majority of those followers and subscribers no longer reside there and so if you were to stay there your audience would simply be your echo.

Believe me when I say history will and has been repeating itself and so as a world changer it's your responsibility to stay up to date and in the know with what's hot and what's not.

Let me shoot out a disclaimer here, this does not mean you go getting into bright shiny object syndrome where you sign up for any and every platform that pops up.

Do your research. Ask your audience. I am constantly polling my people and asking them what they like and where they hang out.

I test different platforms to see, and I ask trend makers. In other words... the teenagers I know.

That's my secret weapon. They are the trend setters for technology.

I remember when Periscope came out, and I missed the first wave opportunity to become an influencer because I didn't know who my ideal client was.

[Remember earlier in the book when I shared that picking an audience is crucial to your success? Just in case you forgot, you can grab your free PDF worksheet at www.irresistibleinyourindustry.com/industryfamousbookbonus]

So I didn't know who my ideal client was and though I occasionally used Periscope, I couldn't stand out as an influencer because my messaging was all over the place.

By the time I figured out who my audience really was and made a decision, I was already around 9 months late.

By then you could clearly see who the influencers in my industry were versus the people who were just giving it a shot.

So I took to my trusted technology insiders –
the TEENS!

I asked them if I should work towards
building my periscope, they looked and me
and straight up said, "nobody wants
Periscope". They told me that they weren't
going to download another app just to see
people go live when they already had apps
like snapchat.

They said they didn't see the purpose of it.

By the way, drop the tomatoes, and don't
shoot the messenger, I am just sharing with
you what they told me.

They said use Instagram.

So I listened.

This was in early 2016, and you know what
happened since? Instagram got the message

and added Live streaming and stories to their platform to compete with snapchat and to in my opinion eliminate the need for Periscope.

And to add insult to injury, a month after me asking them what to do, Facebook rolled out Facebook Live to all it's users – again Periscope in my (and the teenagers') humble opinion became irrelevant.

Do people still use it? Sure, but if you already had a Facebook page with subscribers and followers, why reinvent the wheel.

And even if you don't have a following I would say start there because Facebook allows you to use something called a Pixel, which means you can send ads and other sponsored content to people who have viewed your live videos.

It gives you the opportunity to be a savvy entrepreneur.

This ties in beautifully with the whole concept on monetization because no one wants to be the starving artiste who is changing the world but can't even pay their cell phone bill.

That kind of life is overrated and so unnecessary with the resources we have at our finger tips today.

So I say all this to say that you have to pay attention to what's happening online. People don't live in a bubble. They are social beings and just because you want them to stay in Place A doesn't mean they will. People follow the herd.

We have an innate desire to be accepted and to belong and when you try to force people to stay in isolation away from their tribe, you will be met with great resistance.

So don't fight it, just go with the flow.

Another part of initiative is being able to be fearless.

Some trends are going to come around and are going to cause you to question yourself.

Let's take live streaming for example.

Video isn't new, we've always had video marketing and video sales pages, and video launches, and yes even things like YouTube.

However, the video trend got kicked up a notch when live streaming became mainstream!

Thank you, Periscope, Blab and Meerkat. Even though I expressed my thoughts on such platforms earlier on in this chapter, we must still acknowledge that they changed the game of online video for good.

Yes live streaming existed through platforms such as UStream and Google Hangouts but again, the rise of Periscope, Blab and Meerkat changed the game for good.

And when the game changes you don't run away!

Champions face the music, they adjust, they follow the rules and they win.

Again though, let me throw out this disclaimer – this is not your permission to have bright shiny object syndrome and start downloading a bunch of apps and creating a bunch of accounts.

This however, IS your opportunity to do your research, poll your people, look at your industry, and see where your ideal clients are hanging out and take initiative to be present there.

Once you've built your massive following, gotten all this engagement and credibility, there is only one thing left. This is where you no longer work for someone else. This is where you get to do work you love, change people's lives AND be compensated for it. Let's talk monetization.

The biggest question I get from my clients is "how can I actually make money and reach my financial goals from all the visibility?", and I'm going to say something that may sound weird but you must first realise that....

Making money is easy.

The biggest thing you need to do outside of being the Go-To person is that you need to have something they actually want.

People buy what they want, Full stop!

If you want to get them going from interested to invested where they pay you for your services, you must make sure that what you offer is something they actually want.

It's so simple of a step that people over look it and create unnecessary headaches for themselves trying to be creative and trying to come up with fancy names and services for an irrelevant offer.

Please don't be that person. You deserve to be compensated and when you have the other marketing steps down all you have to do is make a better offer.

Let me solve that for you, just ask yourself:

What do my people want and what are they WILLING to pay for?

It really is that simple.

When your car is running out of gas do you need some sales person to convince you as to why you should buy petrol?

Of course not!

You know you want it and you are willing to buy it. It's call a compelling offer.

So along with all your social media, tribe building, credibility rocking efforts- make sure what you are selling is what they actually are looking to buy.

And in that way, there is no convincing or sleaze necessary.

So that's one fixable mistake that will immediately boost your income from your online efforts. Here's another one:

Your Funnel, Mailing List & The Home Game Advantage

You see the mistake many people make is that they try to focus only on social media. They spend all their efforts thinking about the growth of their social platforms.

And while I am a big advocate of the use of social media, after all, I do give you access to my "From Online Invisible To Social Media Superstar" webinar as one of the bonuses to this book; I am also the first to tell you that there are other ways to boost the reach of social media and monetize your message even more. And that is where the funnel comes in.

Your Funnel

This is one way to go about monetizing your message and is the process by which you take a someone through a sequence or series of steps, and you move them from random stranger, to a member of your tribe and progress them through as actual paying customers.

Sort of like the following image:

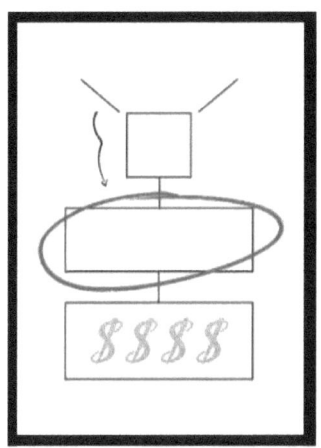

In order to monetize your community, and your message you want to take your audience through a sequence of steps. In the first step, it's all about giving value for free.

Now while you do give value for free on your social platforms and blogs or videos, this is a bit different.

You want to make sure you are giving them something in exchange for their email address.

This is called a "Lead Magnet", and "Opt-In" or a "Freebie".

This is where you give them something juicy that they really want for free in exchange for their email address.

I'm sure you've seen it before, "enter your email and get this free audio", or "enter your email to get access to the webinar" or pdf etc, "enter your name and get 10% off". I'm sure you get the picture.

That is a freebie.

The beautiful thing about the freebie is that now they are a part of your own personal community, and this is where you build a relationship with them and follow up with them to move them from interested, to invested.

Somebody say Cha-ching!

I actually have a PDF roadmap called the "Client Getting Roadmap" where I go in-depth in the previous diagram and show you what each step is and what to do to move your audience from not knowing you, to actually investing in your services.

You can grab that along with your other book bonuses over at www.irresistibleinyourindustry.com/industryfamousbookbonus

I even throw in a bonus audio too where I walk you through the steps so make sure you grab that bonus if you really want the monetization/ client getting road map.

Mailing List

Now let's talk a little bit more about the whole email list shebang and why this is super important.

You see it's something I like to call it the "home game advantage". Remember in the Initiative chapter when I spoke about Myspace and how everyone migrated from using it?

Well what if that happened tomorrow with Facebook, or YouTube or Instagram or whatever platform you are currently using?

What would happen to your influence? What would happen to all those people who followed you? What would happen to your business?

You just lost it all.

And this my friend is why having an email list is so important, especially to monetizing your message.

The thing is even if these platforms don't shut down any time soon, please know that every single month they are updating their algorithms and changing their rules and these can directly impact your reach.

However, if you are able to email your list and send them great content and value, no one can take that away from you.

I have seen in the past where Facebook blocked people from their own groups, or even stopped people from going live to their audience that they worked months to build.

What if that were to happen to you whether on Facebook or on another platform.

It happens every single day.

And if your audience can't hear your message, then monetization is going to be very hard.

So, my homework to you here is to start building a mailing list alongside your social platforms. There are tons of platforms to help you do this from Mailchimp all the way up to more robust systems like Infusionsoft depending on your budget and your reach.

I help my clients walk through this entire process, and I share some of it with you in the client getting road map book bonus.

Implementing these steps helps you to create consistent income in your business and be in full control of your message and your reach without having to feel slighted by social media platforms and their changing algorithms.

What's Next

Now you are equipped with the first steps to help you get the ball rolling so you skyrocket your impact and influence online so you become the go-to expert in you field.

However, there truly is only one thing that can stop you now. And that's you.

This is where the second half of the Industry Fame Formula™ comes in: The Mindset.

The Industry Fame Formula ™

PART 2 – The Mindset

Mindset

Fact: Many people never start.

Fact: Many people start and then they quit.

Fact: It all begins and ends in your mind.

You see, for a lot of world-changers, this phenomenon of never living up to their full potential is steeped in the beliefs of not enough, fear of judgement, fear of failure and even fear of success.

These beliefs started from childhood back in the day when many of us heard children should be seen and not heard.

For others it came from those days growing up where maybe you would laugh or be active and people would say sit down and be quiet, you talk too much.

Many world-changers heard things like "You're too much" or "you're a show off" or "you think you're better than others".

For some however the message was that they were never enough. "Not smart enough", "not pretty enough", and the list could go on.

You see for a child whether it was that they were told they didn't know enough or they were less than or whether they heard they were too much, **the feeling at the end of the day is the same.**

It's the feeling of I don't belong, I don't fit in, I can't be myself it's not safe.

This feeling is what follows many people with potential all the way through adulthood and keeps them stuck in that feeling of playing small. It's that major sabotage that keeps them on the brink of success but never quite there.

It's that feeling that causes some to dream big but never experience it because they squint and hide, and shrink.

It's that recurring voice from childhood saying don't be as big. Don't take as much room.

You see from what I've found working with my clients, that recurring voice can come from anyone.

Maybe it was the teacher who made you feel stupid or slow.

Maybe kids in the class or your crush would laugh at you so you thought let me just not say anything ever again.

Maybe you were outgoing or outspoken and you were getting all the awards and you were the high achiever and people would be jealous and mean and say unkind things to you.

Both scenarios cause feelings of: **you don't belong, you're not enough, you don't deserve it, you're not worthy**.

It truly is an emotional and mental prison.

And so even as you are about to dive into your epic life, know that these little recurring voices will surface. They will try to derail you and sabotage you. Don't let them.

Remember, think, realize and know that you are no longer that seven-year-old child anymore.

You are now a powerful adult with a message and a purpose and a calling and it's your time.

And I know it doesn't mean that those little kids aren't now big bullies who manifest themselves as trolls and haters online.

Yes, they still exist.

But you are not that seven-year-old kid anymore. You are a powerful world-changer with a message and mission and a dream and a vision and a goal and a calling upon your life that needs to be experienced in the world.

So as you embark on this journey to be legendary, it's time for you to **realize that it's okay to be seen.**

It's okay to be heard. It's okay to be visible and to be yourself.

Yes, you may lose some friends along the way. But, they will be replaced believe me, they will be replaced.

God is going to provide you with everything you need and more to get the job done.

This my friend is why you are reading this book today.

Maybe you've skimmed through the rest of the book, but in this moment today, you are reading these words because this message is meant for you.

Remember:

It's okay for you to be seen.

It's safe for you to be seen.

I want you to really acknowledge that.

You see I had my own struggle with this in the past. I saw people in my past who were successful and because they were successful people envied them. And they were killed.. they lost their lives.

That taught me subconsciously that if I was successful to the highest level or if I got visible, or if people knew about what I was doing in the world they would kill me.

I thought it was not safe to be visible, it was not safe to be seen, it was not safe to be heard, it was not safe to be out there – go hide in the bathroom somewhere, go play small.

No wonder I spent the time at that conference hiding in the bathroom.

That recurring voice, though subconscious, said: Don't let people see your light. Because they will hurt you.

You see we all have our "thing", maybe for you it's not being told you're not enough. It could be something else.

For me, I wasn't necessarily bullied or told I wasn't good enough, I had times when people told me you're too much but having the parents I did those things didn't bother me much.

However, knowing someone you loved, who was successful, and losing them because someone else was envious of their success – that bothered me and I didn't even know it was there.

For a long time it really held me back from being who I was meant to be.

I would become shy with some things, even though I am a full-blown extrovert.

I would upload the video then delete it.

I would post the content then delete it or write the post and then don't even post it.

That was my reality.

I was on the verge of being legendary, and every time I took 1 step forward, it's like I would take 2 steps back.

That had nothing to do with my marketing or strategy.

That was all in my head!

However, don't lose faith.

I want you to understand if I can overcome it and if I can go from hiding in a bathroom to having a community of thousands of women from every walk of life all across this globe and if I can be writing books, hosting live events, running massive webinars and touching lives and encouraging people and teaching them...

SO CAN YOU.

Right now I get to be the catalyst for the catalysts. But before I thought it wasn't safe to be visible. I thought it wasn't ok to be seen.

Today however, I am sure I can be visible, I am sure I can be seen and that's all because I worked through all the "stuff" and limiting beliefs that were really holding me back.

It's your time.

Yes it's possible for you, I see these leaps and breakthroughs in my clients all the time, and there is no reason you can't have those breakthroughs too.

Get to the root of your mindset stuff, and that will be the key thing to help you create lasting success!

Conclusion/Summary

So Rockstar, you've made it to the end, and I hope by now you not only see why being #IndustryFamous™ is your number 1 responsibility if you plan on changing the world, but now I hope you also have the formula of exactly how to go about doing it AND being paid too by using the internet.

To sum it all up, the Industry Fame Formula™ is a combination of the powerful mindset work, along with effective marketing techniques. With these 2 together you become not only Irresistible in Your Industry but also Unstoppable in your Industry.

To master your marketing, you must first create a tribe, a group of people who want what you have to offer and who can connect with you and your message.

You must then ensure you build a reputation stronger than titanium wherein you not only build your credibility, but you also reinforce it through consistency and mastery.

A true world-changer understands the voice of the people... their people. They engage and connect on a true heart felt level versus being so far above that they become un-relatable. This true connection is the key to lasting engagements and becomes the place where you don't just create raving fans, but you create brand advocates and evangelists who believe in what you do and begin to even promote you to the people they trust. This is the compounding effect of effective engagement.

To be that go-to person it's your responsibility to keep your ear to the ground and use initiative and creativity to ensure you are serving the people who need you most from where they are at.

And one of the plus sides of being #IndustryFamous™ which is different than just regular "fame" is that you have the blessing of being able to monetize. The opportunity to be paid for being you, and to be paid for work you love.

And while most of the book really delved into some tips and tricks for being effective in your marketing efforts, I want to reinforce that second half of the Industry Fame Formula™.

This is the part that sabotages many people and creates that dreaded 1 hit wonder syndrome instead of creating the legend status that you desire.

It's the mindset work.

It's the mindset of knowing that you are enough and knowing that you CAN create life on your terms. And knowing that judgement and failure doesn't define you but rather, that you define you.

By embracing that you are more than enough and by embracing your own definitions of success, you get to walk in true happiness, fulfilment and contentment, and that my friend is the true essence of a world-changing rock star!

That is the essence of someone who is truly #IndustryFamous™.

With love, I want to thank you for purchasing this book and I want to encourage you to rise above, and continue your journey of inspiration.

Remember there are people curled up on their bathroom floors praying for the message you have within you to share.

This is your time. It's your time to shine, to take centre stage in your life, to finally create the legacy you were born to embrace.

It's your time to become #IndustryFamous.

With Love,

Shaneil

P.S. If you haven't gotten them yet, don't forget to grab your set of juicy book bonuses that you've received as a gift for getting this book. You can get all your bonuses in one place over at www.irresistibleinyourindustry.com/industryfamousbookbonus

About the Author

Shaneil Stewart is an Online Visibility & Marketing Strategist. She is the founder of The Industry Fame Academy and the CEO of Catalyst Digital Media Company Limited where she works with catalysts, coaches and creatives from over 27 countries across the world helping them to be visible online and creating thriving businesses.

Shaneil is a #1 Best Selling Author, Speaker, Coach, Entrepreneur & Philanthropists and has been feature on The Huffington Post, FOX, ABC, The CW, NBC and is the host of Industry Fame TV.

She started www.irresistibleinyourindustry.com as the place where rock star world-changers on the rise could learn the ins and outs of the online marketing world so they can have a massive reach doing the transformative work they love while being compensated for it through heart centred marketing techniques.

She helps her clients position themselves as the Go-To experts in their field through her Industry Fame Formula™ where she pairs powerful mindset work with effective online marketing techniques.

She is also a Certified Digital Marketing Professional and holds multiple master's degrees, including an MA from the Aalborg University in Denmark and an MSW from the University of Lincoln.

She has studied with some of the most iconic entrepreneurs and influencers online such as Ryan Deiss, T Harv Eker, Frank Kern, Lisa

Sasevich, Jeff Walker, Doreen Virtue, Bill Baren, Gina Devee, Melanie Duncan, Dawn Clark and an array of others and best of all she practices what she preaches when it comes to standing out online.

To learn more about Shaneil go to her personal website at www.shaneil.com.